THE CAPSTONE

The Capstone

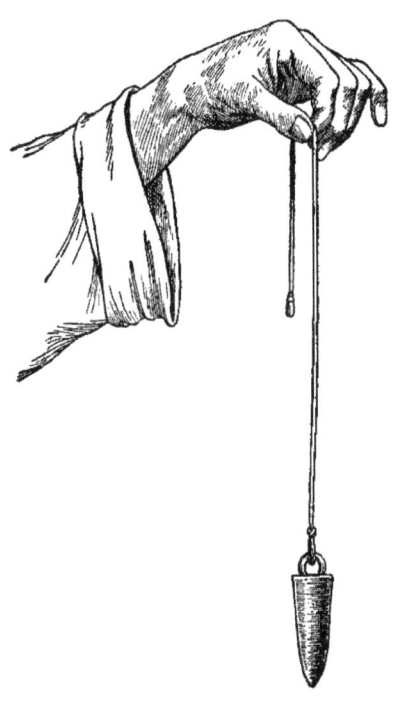

"Behold, the stone that I have set before Joshua, upon this stone are seven eyes. I am opening its inscription says Jehovah of armies. And I will remove the sin of this land in a single day."
Zechariah 3:9

First Edition: 2024
Copyright © 2024 Joshua Stone
Contact: TheFinalKingdom@Yahoo.com
Social Media: E-JW.org

ISBN: 978-1-7370700-8-5

All rights reserved. No part of this publication may be reproduced, stored in a retrieval system, or transmitted in any form or by any means, electronic, mechanical, photocopying, recording, or otherwise, without the author's prior permission.

All Scripture quotations were translated from the original Hebrew, Aramaic, and Greek.

Dedication

This work is dedicated to God Almighty in Christ
Jesus our Lord, through whom all things came to be.

Contents

PREFACE XIII
- Paradise XIV
- The Garden XV
- Darkness XVII

PART ONE 1

A First Day 3
- The Foundation of the World 3
- A Woman 5

A Second Day 7
- Flood Waters 7
- The Tower of Babel 9

A Third Day 11
- Dry Land 11
- The Waters Gathered 14
- The Sanctuary 16
- The Promised Land 20

A Fourth Day 21
The Temple Period 21
Luminaries 23
The Davidic Covenant 25

A Fifth Day 27
Living Creatures 27

A Sixth Day 29
The End of This Age 29
The Lawless One 30

A Seventh Day 33
The Rest 33

PART TWO 35

The Last Days 37

The Lord's Day 39

A Sign in Heaven 41

The Beasts 45
First Beast 45
Second Beast 48

An Open Door 51

Two Witnesses 53

The Capstone 55
Timeline of the End 56

PART THREE 59

The Seven Angels 61

The First Angel 65
First Trumpet 65
First Bowl 67

The Second Angel 69
Second Trumpet 69
Second Bowl 72

The Third Angel 73
Third Trumpet 73
Third Bowl 75

The Fourth Angel 77
Fourth Trumpet 77
Fourth Bowl 78
A Call to Rebuild 79

The Fifth Angel 81
Fifth Trumpet 81
Fifth Bowl 83

The Sixth Angel 85
Sixth Trumpet 85
Sixth Bowl 87

PART FOUR 89

The Seven Thunders 91

The Seventh Angel **95**
Seventh Trumpet - First Thunder 95
Seventh Bowl - Second Thunder 96
First Seal - Third Thunder 97
Second Seal - Fourth Thunder 97
Third Seal - Fifth Thunder 98
Fourth Seal - Sixth Thunder 99
Fifth Seal - Seventh Thunder 99

Forty Days **101**

The Abomination **103**

The Sixth Seal **105**

The Seventh Seal **107**
A Thousand Years 109

New Heavens and New Earth **111**
The Book of Life 113

Preface

Joshua Stone, an ordained minister with over thirty years of experience in scholastic theology and author of *The Final Kingdom,* now brings this timely publication, *The Capstone,* and the finale of this old system of things.

Within, you will discover what precisely to expect at the time of the end, with a detailed chronology of the Revelation of our Lord Christ Jesus.

From the fall of humanity into sin and darkness to the Light that separates the day from night, we will find God has prepared a prophetic roadmap within the first chapter of Genesis to assist His people in understanding metaphors throughout scripture.

See *The Final Kingdom* from your favorite retailer for a detailed breakdown of the Capstone itself.

Paradise

Before us lies a majestic paradise of immense beauty stretching out into all eternity, where all life thrives in harmony and perfection. There are no tears of sorrow, no death or suffering; only joy and compassion, through love, embraced each day. No harm comes to our young children, and no one grows old. Yet we are challenged and engaged by assisting Creation, prospering, and working in unity with all life.

    No one says, "I am alone." And no one ever hungers or thirsts. This paradise before us is real and now arriving. It is ours to protect, and nothing will ever separate us from it again.

The Garden

Before the foundation of the heavens and the earth, God made man. He formed him from the dust of the earth and breathed the breath of life in his nostrils, and the man became a living soul. God placed this first man, Adam, in a garden paradise and provided all things to sustain him. The beauty of the man's garden home and the fulfilling work provided to him were perfect and without blemish.

God also gave the man every tree and plant pleasing to the eyes for food, yet He commanded him not to touch one specific tree in the Garden of Eden. Adam was instructed not to eat from the Tree of the Knowledge of Good and Evil that God had placed in the center of the garden, for if he did, he would die in that day.

And through the fine work provided by his God Jehovah, Adam was found to be an astute observer of all his surroundings. As he observed all of God's Creation, he named all the beasts of the earth and birds of the sky and was joyful before the Lord.

Now, after some time alone in the garden, Jehovah prepared to create a companion for Adam. Causing a deep sleep to fall over the man, God took a rib from Adam and formed a complement to him, and Adam called her *woman*, for out of man, she was created.

God made both man and woman to live in harmony with and rule over Creation in love and peace. Humanity would have free will to accomplish all their hearts' desires, as long as they allowed their Father to guide them. And humanity lived with their God Jehovah in paradise and in solidarity with all Creation.

Darkness

Shortly after the woman's creation, a serpent addressed her near the center of the garden and asked if God had really said not to eat of the Tree of the Knowledge of Good and Evil. This serpent was a son of the living God and a spirit angel who had become proud and haughty, wanting to become like Jehovah, claiming man's worship for himself. And when the Father was away, he spoke to the woman, twisting God's words in an attempt to persuade her to disobey by eating from the tree they had been commanded not to eat from.

    Then the woman confirmed God's words by saying they could eat from every tree but this one. Declaring that God had not been honest with her by saying she would die, the serpent claimed instead that God was keeping knowledge from her that would make her equal to Him. Looking upon the tree as something desirable, she elected to determine right and wrong for herself, and took a fruit from the tree and ate it. She then gave a portion to the man Adam, who was with her, and he ate as well.

When their Father returned, He searched but could not find them, for they were hiding. They hid because they were now aware of their nakedness, the exposed condition of their sin, and because of their disobedience. Their Father asked, "Who has told you, you are naked? Have you eaten from the tree that I commanded you not to eat?" The man blamed his sin on the woman that God had brought to him, and the woman blamed the serpent who deceived her. And through their disobedience, a deep chasm of darkness entered the world, the darkness of sin and death.

However, God loved humanity and did not wish His purpose for them to be lost. So through a deceleration, He promised a Light that would conquer the darkness of night and once again return humanity to that paradise lost. And the Light came into the world and shone before mankind, bringing an end to the darkness; and through Him, eternal paradise is now at hand!

Part One

A First Day

3966–2966 BCE

The Foundation of the World

In the beginning, God looked upon the void of this world after man's fall and determined to bring light into it to separate the day from night, now that the darkness of sin had become part of life on earth. So the Father decided upon seven days to bring an end to the darkness; however, as a day to Him is as a thousand years to man, there would be seven thousand years of God's plan to remove evil from the world forever. And in this time, He would gather many to Himself to learn of His love and see that day when darkness was no more.

God so loved humankind that He chose His own firstborn Son as the foundation of the world to bring about the end of all evil. As the light of mankind, the Son shines in the darkness to light the path of righteousness. It is through Him all those by faith are saved.

Now God turned His attention to that serpent in the garden who had persuaded the first humans to sin and delivered a curse and condemnation upon it. There would be hatred between the serpent and the woman and between its offspring and hers. Just as the woman Eve would be the mother of humanity, so would a woman represent God's means by which He would bring about the redemption of many. This spiritually metaphoric woman, foreseen in the condemnation of the serpent, would give birth to a Son, who would crush the serpent's head as it bites Him on the heel. This male child born of the spiritual woman would give His perfect life on behalf of the many and, at that moment, would seal the fate of the serpent, condemning it to death.

A Woman

This spiritual woman through whom would come an end to the darkness upon the earth, gave birth to the Word who was chosen by God from the beginning. As the Word, Christ Jesus, presented Himself through water and Spirit baptism to do His Father's Will, He offered His own life on behalf of many when dying an unwarranted death at the hands of the world. This selfless act of love and compassion stands as the shining example of how God so loved the world of mankind.

Before all things, the very envisage of the eternal Father became Life. As the intent of God to create, the Word came to be. And the Word was Life. All things came into being through the Word, and without Him, nothing came into being that was through Him. He is Life, and the Life is the Light of mankind.

Within God's plan at the founding of the world, He foreordained an elect to rule alongside the Word in the separation of the day from night. Just as through the rib of Adam, the first man, Eve, the mother of humanity, came to be, so too through the piercing of the second Man, Christ Jesus, a spiritual woman was born as the Bride of Christ. A select number of shining luminaries from humanity would bring the light of God's Word unto the world in preparation for His coming to collect His bride at the end of this age.

A Second Day

2966–1966 BCE

Flood Waters

As mankind had begun to multiply upon the earth during this second day, so had darkness; all inclinations of man's heart were continually evil. Violence and depravity had become the way of life on earth. Many angels, the spirit sons of God, also had forsaken their Creator by falling into sin and iniquity and taking wives from among man, perverting the natural laws of Creation.

So the Father determined to wipe clean the earth from the violence and wickedness that had permeated it. He would cause a separation of the waters above from the waters below, and He called that separation heaven. Whereas at one time the angelic realm had walked freely upon the earth, the creation of heaven now served as a barrier between the waters of the spirit sons of God from the waters making up humanity. So God caused a great flood to wipe clean that world of old.

A remnant, however, would pass through those floodwaters in an ark God directed a man named Noah to build, saving himself and his family. Noah was faithful in all God had instructed him by collecting the world's animals and building the ark to protect them from the deluge so they could rebuild and repopulate after those floodwaters had receded. And when the ark came to rest upon a high mountain, Noah and his family and all the animals they had protected within moved out upon the earth once again. Then God blessed Noah and his sons and told them to multiply and replenish the whole earth.

Just as in the days of Noah, so will the end of the sixth day be. For people will be lovers of themselves, rather than lovers of God. And they will take no note until fire comes and sweeps them all away. However, a faithful remnant will pass through those fires, be cleansed through their faith in Christ Jesus, and enter a land prepared for them from the founding of the world.

The Tower of Babel

As humanity began to replenish the earth after the deluge of Noah's day, they gathered as one in defiance of God in a land named Shinar. Rather than going out to fill and subdue the entire earth, they came together to fulfill their own desires in contradiction to the Lord's instructions.

Although the heavens served to separate the angelic and earthly realms, the darkness of evil was still to influence humankind through the craftiness of that serpent from the Garden of Eden. And herein lies the deception of that liar in the garden: The accuser and adversary of God's people known as the satan presents himself as an angel of light. This liar and murderer of man uses deception by appearing to bring humanity together in peace and security, yet without the Creator of life.

The satan, desiring a place and throne above God Himself, began to influence those in the land of Shinar to construct a tower to reach the heavens. As a symbol of defiance of God's commands, this tower made of fired clay bricks would serve as the defining example of false worship in the boastful proclamation of humanistic accomplishments.

As the birthplace of an oppositional spiritual woman who tries to thwart God's plan to bring about light through His woman, the land of Shinar would become the mother of religious harlotry and the cause of all the shed blood on earth. Idolatrous worship of humanistic ideologies had its birth at that tower.

So when God saw that mankind was coming together in opposition to His Will, He determined to disperse humanity across the entirety of the globe by confusing their singular language into multiple languages. And from then on, that city became known as Babel.

And as humanity began to spread throughout the world, they took their ideologies and false worship adopted within the land of Shinar and carried these to all the far reaches of the earth.

A Third Day

1966–966 BCE

Dry Land

As mankind left off building the city of Babel and began to spread throughout the earth, God determined to collect people together under His name. Through His servants from Abraham to David, their God Jehovah would gather chosen waters of humanity to a promised land and mountain He would call Zion. And by separating life-giving waters unto Himself, He left the waves and wind to drive the turbulent oceans of the rest of humanity that God called seas.

As the waters divided at the Red Sea and dry land appeared, God protected His people from their enemies. So, too, as the waters of the Jordan halted and the ark stood on dry ground, Jehovah God would bring His people into a promised land.

During this third day from the founding of the world, God collected His waters through the seed of a man named Abram. And God promised Abram He would gather his offspring to a land He showed him in the location of Canaan, a land flowing with the abundances of life. However, first Abram's seed would wander in a land not their own, serving others for a period of time.

There would be four hundred and thirty years from the day God promised a singular seed through Abraham that would bring blessings to all nations, till the Israelites' exit from captivity in the land of Egypt. And this promise was given to Abraham in a sacrifice narrative foreshadowing God's Son when Abraham offered up his twelve-year-old son Isaac by God's direction on Mount Moriah. And when God halted Abraham's actions, He promised Abram that his future offspring would possess the gates of the enemy through a seed that would bring blessings to many. Then there would be four hundred years from Abraham's death to his offspring entering the Promised Land.

Jehovah's waters of people would have a tumultuous journey in the keeping of their covenants before God. However, just as a seed produces vegetation of the field and fruit-bearing trees, so too would the knowledge of the Father begin to grow in the land during this time. There would be many fine works from faithful men and women who came to know their God and Father Jehovah.

The Waters Gathered

After a great famine fell upon the earth, the offspring of Abraham, who would be known as the Israelites through the patriarch Jacob, would find themselves in captive slavery to Egypt. So God chose a man named Moses to bring His people Israel out of Egypt to the land of Canaan He had promised their forefather, Abraham. God caused many signs and wonders through the two prophets Moses and Aaron before the pharaoh of Egypt to force the king to release His people.

After the Egyptian pharaoh capitulated to God's demand to let His people go, Moses led the chosen people out of Egypt; however, regretting this decision, Pharaoh and his army pursued the Israelites to recapture them. And as Moses raised his hand over the Red Sea, God caused the waters to split and dry land to appear, allowing God's people to pass safely across the dry ground their God had provided.

However, at the place of Mount Sinai, the Israelites became involved in apostasy. Believing Moses was delayed when in the mountain before God, they built an idol of gold resembling a calf and began worshiping it instead of their God Jehovah. And when Moses came down from the mountain with the tablets of the Law of God and saw all that the Israelites were doing, he smashed the tablets before them, destroyed their idol, and many fell slain by the sword.

Because of the Israelites' apostasy, Jehovah God determined that their generation would not enter His promised land. So God caused the Israelites to live a nomadic life, wandering in the wilderness for forty years.

The Sanctuary

God gave Moses detailed instructions to construct a sanctuary that would play a leading role in Jehovah's plan to end darkness upon the earth. This sanctuary structure would serve as a shadow or metaphor for God's plans to bring about His Will on earth. It would consist of a two-room tent surrounded by a courtyard draped by fine linen.

Within this structure is found a virtual map of prophetic markers that correspond to the eternal salvation of humanity. An outer courtyard draped in pure white linen surrounded the tabernacle within, representing a cleansed state of those entering, spiritually clothed in white garments to cover the shameful nakedness of sin. However, to enter the inner court, one needed to pass through the outer curtain gate of red, blue, and purple, representing the Lord Christ Jesus, the only path unto righteousness and the forgiveness of sin.

In the courtyard center was the altar of burnt sacrifice and the laver. Those entering would offer their sacrifices upon the altar, as a shadow of the Lord Christ Jesus's sacrifice for the forgiveness of their sin. Chosen as the sacrificial Lamb before the world's founding, the Lamb of God would bring everlasting forgiveness of sin to humanity, in fulfillment of the lamb that was offered on the brazen altar by the Israelites in the courtyard of the sanctuary.

Just beyond the brazen altar, the priests would wash in the water laver as a cleansing before entering the sanctuary itself. Made from the mirrors donated by the women of Israel, this laver reminds us that a reflection within is necessary for the recognition of sin.

The tabernacle itself was adorned with another red, blue, and purple gate representing our Lord, which closed off two rooms beyond. Entering the first room, known as the Holy Place, the priests would take care of the functions and duties within. Over time, these priests would come to represent an elect chosen from the world's founding under a new covenant arrangement in Christ to serve with Him over the kingdom of God. Just as these priests served before the Lord in a physical sanctuary on earth, this first room represented the future work of apostles of Christ Jesus in service of God's kingdom on earth.

To their right was the table of showbread with one loaf from each of the twelve tribes of Israel, a shadow of the future 144,000 elect who would serve as priests alongside the Lord in His kingdom.

To the left stood a candlestick of seven lamps representing the Word of God itself. Just as this lamp lighted the way for the priests within the Holy Place, so too God's words bring the light of understanding before man.

And at the back of this first room sat the altar of burnt incense. As the smoke rose from the incense offered upon it, it passed through an opening in the top of the curtain separating the Holy Place from the Most Holy Place beyond; these representing the prayers of the elect coming before God the Father Himself.

Once a year, on the remembrance day of Yom Kippur, the high priest would enter the Most Holy Place through another curtain of red, blue, and purple with the blood of a sacrifice to present before the mercy seat of the ark within. This remembrance day would serve as a foreshadowing of when the Lord Christ Jesus would present Himself before Jehovah God and receive the kingdom of the earth at the end of the sixth day.

The Promised Land

As the people prepared to cross into the land promised to their ancestor Abraham after spending forty years wandering the wilderness, the priests stood at the edge of the Jordan River with the Ark of God as the waters were stopped and dry land appeared for them to cross. Thus, the people of God crossed over into the land of Canaan.

As the Israelites began to multiply in the Promised Land, they settled at Mount Moriah, the location God had pledged to the patriarch Abraham and his seed. They commenced construction of a permanent city named Jerusalem and fulfilled God's plan to gather the waters of His people to the land He promised in this third day from the beginning.

A Fourth Day

966 BCE–35 CE

The Temple Period

Beginning this fourth day, God chose King Solomon to build the permanent temple structure in Jerusalem. During this time known as the Temple Period, Jehovah brought about lights and luminaries through His prophets, such as Daniel, to bring the understanding of times and seasons to His people.

God set up remembrance days of fasting and feasts to be kept at their appointed times and serve as markers within the lunar–solar calendar to fulfill His Will. These prophetic lights were designated as signs and seasons for when the holy days would separate the light from the darkness in the very days and years of their fulfillment. They mark the exact time through the lunar–solar calendar when God's festival seasons will have their ultimate completion. From the founding of the world, the fulfillment of God's plans is portrayed through the events observed within His remembrance days.

At the close of this fourth day, God made two great lights. He made the greater to rule the day, and the lesser to rule the night. The spiritual woman foreseen in the garden, clothed with the sun and with the moon at her feet, gives birth to the Son, Christ Jesus, the bright Morning Star that shines before humanity and that great Light bringing healing rays to all those who exercise faith in Him. And established through Him are the faithful priests who shine like stars in the darkness of this world, bringing lights of understanding to God's people.

The woman who gives birth to the Son is governed by the days and years fulfilled in their times and seasons to bring about God's Will and the final judgment on darkness through His remembrance holy days. And through His prophets, He presents those days and years to the world.

Luminaries

During the Israelites' captivity in Babylon, God gave His prophets day counts to mark the periods between the fulfillments of these remembrance days. As the lunar calendar expands and contracts in concordance with the solar, the day counts between each holy day vary depending on the times studied. However, only one time in history do the holy days yet to be fulfilled line up with the chronology set out in Scripture.

When the Word and Morning Star, Christ Jesus, completed His ministry upon the earth, He fulfilled the spring holy days of Passover, unleavened bread, firstfruits, and Pentecost on the very days of their occurrence. Still yet to be fulfilled within the sixth day are the fall holy days of Yom Teruah, Yom Kippur, and Sukkot. At the end of the six thousand years from the founding of the world, these holy days will be fulfilled by the return of the Lord Christ Jesus when He brings God's kingdom to earth, separating the Light of God from the darkness of sin and death.

The Davidic Covenant

The Lord God does nothing without first revealing to His prophets what is to occur. And such was the case when God gave the prophet Daniel a seventy-year prophecy to assist the Israelites in determining the exact year when the Messiah was to appear before them. In a vision given to him, Daniel was told there would be seventy weeks of years from the call to rebuild the walls of Jerusalem to the coming of the Messiah, the Leader. And to the very day and year set out through the lunar–solar calendar, Christ Jesus was baptized in fulfillment of the Davidic covenant, a promise of an eternal king from the line of David.

As the seventieth week began at Christ's baptism, that covenant for the Messiah was held in place for the Israelite nation for seven years. And at the half of that seventieth-week, sacrificial gift offerings at the temple ceased when Christ Jesus became the one True Sacrifice, establishing the reality in Himself.

Fulfilling a prophecy given to the prophet Jeremiah many centuries previously, Christ Jesus fulfilled the High Priest role when He returned to heaven and presented His blood before His God and Father Jehovah. When God spoke to Jeremiah, the old ways were obsolete and ready to pass. And after the realities were fulfilled in the Messiah, the physical shadow temple on earth no longer functioned and ceased to have any further place in God's prophetic plans.

Ending this seventieth week of Daniel's prophecy, a Roman Centurion named Cornelius and his family were baptized through the Holy Spirit, at which point no longer was being the offspring of Abraham a matter of genetics in prophecy, but rather one of faith through Christ. All who profess the Lord Christ Jesus as their Savior and King are the children of Abraham and heirs to the promise.

Keep the Lord's commands and remain clean from the vileness of this world, dear friends, and you will receive the free gift of life.

A Fifth Day

35–1035 CE

Living Creatures

During this fifth day from the foundation of the world, God made living creatures through His Spirit that swarm the waters of the sea of mankind. As the gospel of God's kingdom spread throughout the world during this period, many Spirit-born Christians, great and small, multiplied within the seas of humanity. Just as Adam became a living soul through the breath of life from God, so too is everyone in Christ born again through Spirit and water baptism.

Christ Jesus sent out the faithful surrounding Him as fishers of men to all nations. Spreading out into all the world, they bring spiritual life to everyone exercising faith in Him. As those chosen from the world's founding assist in bringing many from the waters of humanity to life, they soar like eagles as they call for repentance from sin and announce the coming judgments upon the earth at the arrival of God's kingdom.

A Sixth Day

1035–2035 CE

The End of This Age

At the end of this age, when the harvest is ripe, the Lord will gather His elect from the four corners of the earth, raising them as spirit creatures in His image to rule with Him over all His kingdom. They govern to separate light from darkness, good from evil, and assist all life to grow and prosper. Over a thousand years, God's kingdom on earth will return all life to perfection and harmony.

Ending the sixth day, the world's armies gather against the Lord Christ Jesus as He appears before them all in the clouds of heaven. Herein lies the faith of the holy people—the ones who endure until the end are saved.

The Lawless One

The lawless one who will come against God's people will be revealed as a governmental agency and work in the way the satan works. Claiming to have humanity's best interest in mind, this entity will intend to bring about regulatory change requiring membership into a religious conglomerate organizational arrangement to continue sacrifices of praise—those who accept this association take upon themselves the mark of the beast of apostasy. This regulation represents a humanistic attempt to bring people together separate from God's Will and direction. It will be the catalyst for recognizing the image of the collective governmental religious agency and identifying this false prophet organization claiming to bring goodwill. At that point, the time of the end and the day of the Lord have come.

This human desire to come together separate from God's Will had its founding in the city of Babel and has continued to permeate all aspects of society since. Just as the satan masquerades as an angel of light, so too will this end-time push of support for this religiosity agency by God's people be presented as an inclusive, equitable regulation to better humanity. However, in reality, only God's kingdom will bring peace and safety to this world, and all those supporting this image of the beast depart from the holy covenant of God.

May all through faith remain in God's grace and ever more so as the day draws near.

A Seventh Day

2035–3035 BCE

The Rest

On the seventh day, God rests from all His works of bringing about the separation of light from the darkness. Blessed are all those who enter His rest through the blood of the Lamb; theirs is the kingdom of God.

Be on guard, you faithful, for the serpent will be let loose before the completion of this day to deceive once again, causing many to fall into darkness and be cut off forever.

Part Two

The Last Days

This is the Revelation God gave Christ Jesus to show His people the things that must shortly take place in the last days, or time of the end. He made this Revelation known by sending an angel to His servant John, who wrote down what he saw for future generations of God's faithful.

In the last days of this world's system of things, two prophets of God will have the work of announcing the final judgments upon those in opposition to God's kingdom. Through the fulfillment of prophecies in their appointed times, these two witnesses will announce the coming of God's kingdom during the final seven-year period of the sixth day, as the events within the revelation to John begin to unfold.

Through the repentance of sin by faith in Christ Jesus and the keeping of God's commandments, humanity is invited into the Lord's final seventh-day kingdom that will put an end to all sin and death. *To Him who loves us and gave His Life on our behalf so that we might live by Him, be all power and glory forever and ever. May all Creation glorify and testify to our Father's glory through Christ Jesus. Amen.*

Listen to what our Lord says: "Behold, I stand at the door and knock. If anyone hears My voice and opens the door, I will enter to them, and dine with them, and they with Me. Those who conquer, I will grant them to sit with Me on My throne, as I also conquered and sat down with My Father on His throne. The one who has an ear, let them hear what the Spirit says to the churches" (Revelation 3:20–22).

John wrote down all of these things in a letter and sent it to the Seven Churches of Asia Minor. What follows here is a chronological record of the vision John recorded that will take place in the last days.

The Lord's Day

While on the island of Patmos, on account of the preaching work, John was keeping the remembrance of our Lord's Day when through God's Spirit he heard a voice as a trumpet behind him speaking. And it said to him, "Write down what you see and send it to the Seven Churches of Asia Minor."

Turning to see the one speaking to him, he saw seven golden lampstands representing those seven churches. Within the lampstands, John saw the Lord Christ Jesus, and He was holding seven stars, representing the seven angels of those seven churches. And John recorded that His eyes were like flaming torches, as these represent His foresight of the coming judgments upon the world.

The flaming eyes of the Lord are inscribed upon the top stone of God's Word in fulfillment of the times and seasons in the last days. His face shines like the sun, scorching all who refuse to repent—yet bringing the light of salvation to those saved through His grace. From His mouth, a two-edged sword, His Word, goes out in judgment at the appointed time.

As John looked upon the Lord Christ Jesus, he fell faint at His feet; and as the Lord touched John, He said, "Fear not, I am the First and the Last, and the Living One. I died, and behold, I am alive forever, and I have the keys of Death and Hades. Write down the things you have seen and these things that will take place after this" (Revelation 1:17–19).

A Sign in Heaven

Suddenly, John saw a great sign in heaven—a woman clothed in the sun with the moon at her feet and twelve stars on her head. This woman is the same one whom God prophesied from the beginning in the Garden of Eden. She is the means by which He brings about His final separation of the light from the darkness. Being clothed in the sun with the moon at her feet, she is governed by the lunar–solar calendar and fulfilled through the appointed times of the festival seasons set up through God's prophets of old. The twelve stars about her head represent the 144,000 elect who will rule alongside the Lord in His kingdom.

In John's vision, this woman is pregnant and about to give birth to a male child. And as that birth is fulfilled in our Lord's earthly ministry, a terrible dragon is seen standing before the woman, wishing to devour the child. However, the Lord Christ Jesus conquered the dragon, the satan and liar, and was snatched away to God the Father after His faithful sacrifice on behalf of mankind.

At His Ascension, our Lord fulfilled the High Priest role and became the realities that were the shadow within the old covenant. Completed in Christ Jesus were all aspects of the Law. No longer did a physical temple building harbor the Spirit of God, but rather God's Spirit came to reside with those who maintain faith in Him. No longer would God's people offer a daily sacrificial animal in a physical courtyard; their preaching and praise of God's name now became the reality in prophecy. All of God's people clothed in white robes cleansed in the blood of the Lamb now make up the real courtyard on earth.

Our Lord's earthly preaching work represented the first half of the seventieth week of years as presented through the prophet Daniel. Upon Christ's return to His Father at His Ascension, war broke out in heaven. The dragon and its angels battled against the Lord and His angels, and the Lord defeated the dragon and threw it and its angels down to the earth. And when the dragon saw it had been thrown down, it went off to pursue the woman and her offspring; those keeping the testimony and faith in Christ. At which point, as seen by John in the Lord's Revelation, the woman flees into the wilderness for the last half of that seventieth week or 1,260 days. The woman's offspring were indeed in the wilderness during this time, as they faced dangers and persecutions from all around them.

    Though the dragon continually attempted to overcome the woman's seed through the persecuting waters of turbulent mankind, the Lord God provided the sustaining Bread of Life from heaven and the oil of His Word to light their paths.

The Beasts

First Beast

Next in his vision, John sees the dragon that had been thrown down to the earth standing on the edge of the tumultuous seas of mankind. And as he looks on, he sees a beast coming out of that sea. This beast has seven heads and ten horns, with ten crowns on those horns. Its body resembles animals like those presented to Daniel of old, representing a succession of nation-states. It looks like a leopard with a bear's paws and a lion's mouth. With these animals now combined into one from the seas of humanity, this beast becomes a conglomerate earthly organization, unlike all previous to it. It exercises authority but not through its own power; it relies on the might and strength of its individual nation heads to enforce this conglomerate organization's recommendations.

John is about to hear this beast speaking boastfully from its lion's mouth. Masquerading as an angel of light to deceive, this first beast will speak of solidarity against many of the challenges and trials before humanity, without any mention of God's kingdom. It will boast of its own intentions to bring peace and prosperity among all societies, while in its heart it intends world domination. Just as the boastful words of King Nebuchadnezzar of Babylon, and the people from Babel of old, these haughty words originate from how the satan works.

As John looks on, he notices that one of this beast's heads appears to have a fatal wound that had healed. Similar to this head wound, when King Nebuchadnezzar of Babylon spoke boastfully of his own pride, he was cut down like a tree, losing his sanity for seven biblical lunar years. It was not until the end of these 2,520 days that Nebuchadnezzar's reason returned to him when he raised his eyes and recognized that Jehovah God rules and puts whom He wishes in places of authority through His Will.

Just as Babylon represented the lion within Daniel's prophecies, this head with the healed wound in John's vision of the end represents Babel of old and its ideological recovery into this lion and the spiritual harlot Babylon the Great. And as the lion's boastful words come on December 28, 2028, this will start the tribulation and countdown of the final seven years of the end. There will be 2,520 days between the boastful words of the lion and when Christ Jesus appears in the clouds of heaven to gather His elect. And there will be exactly seven solar years from these boastful words of Babylon the Great to the first day of God's final kingdom.

However, the apostasy of God's people must be made evident before our Lord's return.

Second Beast

As John looks on, he sees a second beast coming out of the earth. Rather than coming from the seas of mankind among land already founded, this beast comes from a part of the earth not previously established. This beast has two horns like a lamb, containing two nation-states in one. Though it acts as a peacemaker, it speaks as a dragon. Working as if it has humanity's best interest in mind, it hides behind its true intent like a wolf in sheep's clothing. This beast from the earth operates as the power behind the first beast, demanding allegiance from all nations to the first conglomerate beast from the sea.

And as John continues his eyewitness of the Revelation of Christ, he sees the second beast performing great signs. As an image of idolatry, it brings about a regulation requiring religious entities to become part of a combined organizational arrangement in violation of God's commands to remain separate from the world. This idolatrous regulation established on December 28, 2028, will represent the signs of the mark of the beast and will bring apostasy on all those supporting these lies and deceit. The satan offered Jesus all the world's kingdoms because he owned them; therefore, do not be seen endorsing these worldly nations; continue supporting God's kingdom.

Just as Solomon took upon himself the mark of 666 by collecting more gold to himself than God had commanded and falling into apostasy, so too will two-thirds of God's people in the time of the end take upon themselves this number of humanistic apostasy. Just as the king of Babylon set up an image measuring 60x6x6 representing idolatry for those not passing through the fire, the ones waiting on the Lord, in the end, are refined by the fire from our Lord's eyes in fulfillment of the appointed times. Rather than setting up a golden calf as the Israelites did in the wilderness after the exile from Egypt, God's people, in the end, are admonished to buy gold refined through fire from our Lord Christ Jesus in continued sacrifices of praise separate from this beast's 666 mark through a united ecclesial agenda.

Do not be deceived by these lying signs and wonders when presented by these nations as being in the majority's best interest. The satan presents himself as an angel of light so that, if possible, he can deceive even the elect of God. However, we are not the sort who will support the dragon's kingdoms on earth, for through faith in God Almighty and His Son Christ Jesus, we are part of that kingdom of God to come that will put an end to all suffering and death and where all faithful humanity will go on to eternal life.

Just as these two beasts are about to act through their boastful words and lying signs, John sees an open door in heaven and a voice like a trumpet calling out to him, saying, "Come up here, and I will show you what must take place after this." (Revelation 4:1).

An Open Door

As John continues to record the Revelation from Christ Jesus, he sees an open door in heaven. And as he looks on, he hears the voice of the angel who came to show him these things call out to him; and at once, John is in the Spirit before the throne of God. He then sees flashes of lightning and hears rumblings of thunder coming out from before the One seated upon the throne. And around the throne are four living creatures covered with the eyes of knowledge and wisdom. John also sees twenty-four elders, dressed in white garments of righteousness and crowns of gold, destined to rule. And before them is mankind as if a sea of glass, clear as crystal.

John is then given a measuring reed and told to measure God's temple, the incense altar, and those worshiping within. Just as the priests in the shadow temple of old had their responsibilities, so too the 144,000 elect have been assigned their work before the Lord during these fifth and sixth days from the founding of the world. And as John measures the temple making up the elect and the altar of their prayers, their number is made ready, and the countdown to the arrival of God's kingdom has begun.

As John goes about his measuring, the angel speaking with him tells him to disregard the sanctuary courtyard, for it is to be handed over to the nations, along with the daily sacrifices within, the preaching work of God's people. When the second beast establishes the idolatrous religious conglomerate, God's organizational arrangement on earth will take upon itself transgression through its acceptance of this unity agenda on September 10, 2029, beginning the 2,300 days till His final kingdom and the new world arrives.

Two Witnesses

Announcing the events to come upon the world will be two prophets of God living in the time of the end. Serving as luminaries before humanity, these two reveal the coming Will of God through the stone with seven eyes of the Lord. As olive trees produce the oil of lamps to see, these two prophets provide the finality of God's Word ahead of time. The eyes upon this stone are the fulfillments of the remembrance days in their appointed times.

Prophetically known as Joshua and Zerubbabel, these two men living in the time of the end will be known through their work before the Lord of the whole earth. Joshua presents the stone with seven eyes, the very Capstone of Scripture itself. These lights of prophetic remembrance days fulfilled in their appointed times go out to and fro into the world, containing the powers of these two prophets in the end. God's Will for bringing about His plan to end sin and death upon the earth is made known through Joshua before its fulfillment comes to fruition in the time of the end. Just as with Moses to Pharaoh of Egypt, so Joshua carries the responsibility of presenting these imminent events to all the earth.

The prophetic Zerubbabel will have the responsibility before the Lord of beginning the construction of the earthly spiritual Jerusalem after its fall deep in the time of the end. Rejoice when you see the stone with the seven eyes of the Lord in the hands of Zerubbabel. For these will roam to and fro as they go out to their completion upon the earth.

As these two begin their earthly preaching work, the love they show from God the Father through Christ their Lord will be evident in their commission of assisting in God's Will of bringing the lights of understanding before humanity in the separation of the light from the darkness. For these two stand alongside the Lord of the whole earth, providing the oil to the lamp of God's Word that shines in His holy temple.

The Capstone

666: December 28, 2028 – Asara B'Tevet

✧

Apostasy: September 10, 2029 – Yom Teruah

✧

Walls Breached: July 6, 2033 – 9th of Tammuz

✧

Temple Destroyed: August 5, 2033 – 10th of Av

✧

State Collapse: October 4, 2034 – Sukkot

✧

Coronation: October 13, 2035 – Yom Kippur

✧

God's Kingdom: December 28, 2035 – Hanukkah

Timeline of the End

(7 Times, 7 Years Begin)
666 Established: December 28, 2028 – Asara B'Tevet

|

(2,300 Days Begin)
Apostasy of God's People: September 10, 2029 – Yom Teruah/Gedaliah

|

(430, 1260, 1290, 1335 Days Begin)
Preaching Given to Babylon: May 2, 2032

|

(430 Days End)
Spiritual Walls Breached: July 6, 2033 – 9th of Tammuz

|

Spiritual Temple's Destruction: August 5, 2033 – 10th of Av

|

(777th Day/70 Weeks Begin)
Call to Rebuild Spiritual Jerusalem: June 17, 2034

(450 Days Begin)
State Collapse: October 4, 2034 – Sukkot

|

(1,260 Days End)
Coronation: October 13, 2035 – Yom Kippur

|

(70 Weeks End)
Two Witnesses Resurrected: October 20, 2035

|

(1,290 Days End)
Abomination: November 12, 2035

|

(7 Times End)
Christ Appears: November 22, 2035

|

(7 Years, 2,300, 1335, 450 Days End)
God's Kingdom: December 28, 2035 – Hanukkah

Part Three

The Seven Angels

As John continues his account of the Revelation of the Lord Christ Jesus, he sees seven angels standing before the throne of God, who are given seven trumpets and seven bowls. And as these seven angels are prepared, we will see that the first four trumpets and bowls pertain to the dispersing of God's people into spiritual captivity to Babylon the Great. And the last three pertain to woes upon the turbulent seas of mankind.

Just then, Joshua enters the courtyard where the Spirit of God is residing, south of the prophetic earthly temple on earth. And as he reaches in among the flames before the glory of the Lord, an angel fills his hands with burning coals of judgments that Joshua is to toss over the city of

Jerusalem, God's spiritual organization on earth. And just when Joshua is given the fire of prophetic fulfillments, an angel grabs fire from the incense altar within the Holy Place and casts it to the earth.

The angel's casting of the fire from the incense altar is in response to the boastful words from the first beast, and the second lawless antichrist beast's established mark of apostasy from God. These will occur on the first remembrance day fulfilled in the end at Asra B'Tevet on December 28, 2028, the beginning of tribulation on earth. As this first flame of the Capstone containing the Lord's eyes is cast to the earth, this begins the last seven years of this sixth day and is seen by John as the sea of mankind mingled with fire.

At this point, the temple of heaven is filled with a cloud of smoke from the glory of God, and no one may enter the sanctuary until all the bowls and trumpets are complete.

There will be great nationalistic support for this united religious regulatory agenda as Christians from all aspects of society begin supporting these lies and deceit, absent of God's Will. Just as did those at the Tower of Babel, these individuals, in the end, who take the mark of the beast of idolatry upon themselves, will be touting their own collective agendas in opposition to God's commands to remain separate from the world.

Through this second beast's actions of establishing religious idolatry, it causes our Lord's response in casting to the earth the fires of his final judgment days. And when you see the manifestation of these lying signs, get out of any spiritual organization supporting such governmental religious-unity agendas. My dear friends, you have been warned: remain in the faith, keep the commands of God, and continue to be separate from the world.

During this time, there will be six others along with Joshua announcing the arrival of this idolatrous mark of the beast. They will call out to those of God's people who mourn the iniquities within the spiritual temple, marking them with the seal of God, as the unfaithful take upon themselves the mark of apostasy.

The First Angel

First Trumpet

As John hears the first angel sound his trumpet, Joshua tosses the fire given him by the angel over the spiritual city of God. This flame from the stone with the Lord's eyes is seen on September 10, 2029, when God's earthly organizational arrangement adopts the beast's idolatrous religious agenda in fulfillment of Yom Teruah. There will be 2,300 days from this moment till God's seventh-day rest and the earthly temple's restoration.

Just as the three friends of Daniel passed through the fiery furnace for refusing to worship the idolatrous image set up in Babylon of old, so too must one-third of Christ's faithful followers be refined and pass through these testing, tempering fires within the time of the end. One-third of God's people will mourn the adoption of the beast's mark by the elders within their churches, refusing to adopt this nationalistic idolatry. Just as the Israelites mourned the killing of Gedaliah, the faithful governor of God who failed to recognize the dangers that lay ahead, so too will these events come upon all the Lord's people unexpectedly.

When you see these things come to be, continue upholding the faith, knowing that the desolation of God's spiritual organization is at hand, for your endurance brings salvation through your refining by fire from the Lord Christ Jesus. Just as seeds in fine soil grow trees producing befitting fruits, our Lord's fiery judgments cause the faithful vegetation and grasses of His people to pass through these refining fires.

First Bowl

As this first angel pours out his bowl upon the earth, spiritual sores and ulcers come upon those who adopt this mark of the beast. Two-thirds within the Lord's earthly organization will accept their elders' decision to adopt this conglomerate religious-equity agenda by touting their misguided support of superior authorities. Believing that this beast of John's vision works on behalf of humanity's best interest, in reality, those professing the faith but yet agreeing with this religious regulatory agenda will be supporting the dragon presenting itself as an angel of light.

There is only one kingdom working on behalf of the true best interest of humanity, and that is God's kingdom. Worship the One who made all things; support His Will, and disregard any agenda to gather together in the guise of peace, separate from God's kingdom.

The Second Angel

Second Trumpet

As John witnesses the second angel sound his trumpet, he sees a great mountain burning with fire thrown into the sea. This spiritual Mount Moriah represents God's organizational arrangement on earth as seen burning from the fire tossed over it by Joshua in conjunction with the Capstone before him.

At this second trumpet on May 2, 2032, the sacrifices of praise are handed over to the wild beasts of the earth. This day marks the courtyard's trampling, beginning 1,260 days before our Lord Christ Jesus receives the kingdom of the earth. There will be 1,290 days from this date until an abomination attacks the Lord's elect on earth, and 1,335 days till the first day of God's final kingdom and His seventh-day rest.

At this point, the sacrifices of praise are given over to the beast, requiring all preachers of God's Word to support this adoption of the mark of apostasy. When the Lord's earthly organization accepts this conglomerate religious-unity agenda, do not turn a blind eye to the disgusting things being done within; remove yourself from this nationalistic idolatry and instead support God's kingdom alone.

Just as John sees the harlot woman, Babylon the Great, drinking from a golden cup full of the blood of the Lord's elect, God's people are seen as blood being spiritually killed and cut off from the courtyard's sacrifices of praise. These living creatures from the sea this mountain had been thrown into are those born of the Spirit from God since the fifth day from the world's founding. Many local churches remain faithful as ships in the sea, choosing to depart and shutter their buildings rather than support these idolatrous adoptions by those in spiritual leadership roles.

The two witnesses, Joshua and Zerubbabel, are now seen by John clothed in sackcloth, a sign of mourning the sacrifices of praise controlled by the wild beast. Although they had been prophesying previously, their announcements of the coming judgments on earth continue as the earthly organization works to further the dragon's intentions from this point on.

Second Bowl

As this second angel pours out his bowl upon the sea, those who support the wild beast's apostasy are the same as dead spiritually. Anyone who supports and encourages others to adopt the dragon's intentions of bringing humanity together under a singular humanistic agenda will be separating themselves from God's grace. And by teaching others to put their faith in human intent rather than in God's kingdom, they will be idolizing nationalistic demon-inspired lies that will lead them to eternal death.

The Third Angel

Third Trumpet

On July 6, 2033, the third angel will sound his trumpet. And in fulfillment of the prophetic ninth of Tammuz, the earthly organization that once represented God's Will will be breached on this date. Nations will come against this group, investigating wrongdoing and illegal actions of its leaders, breaking through its whitewashed walls. Its highly publicized transgressions will cause great reproach and blasphemy against the Almighty's Holy Name.

As one of the stars in our Lord's hands, the angel of the Church of Laodicea falls into world news, as this church becomes bitter to the palate. And as John saw this star fall on a third of the waters of God's people, these died metaphorically as this church's wrongdoings became evident in fulfillment of the Capstone's third fiery eye of the Lord on the ninth of Tammuz.

All those in Christ must maintain your faith and hope through these trying times and know your God sends you the helper of His Spirit as you endure. Know that your faith is being refined and whitened for the appointed time of the end.

Third Bowl

As the third angel pours out his bowl on the rivers and waters of the Lord's Church, they become blood. Those who supported the idolatries now become blood before the nations they endorsed. On July 6, 2033, Babylon the Great will turn on the leaders within God's organizational arrangement that took upon themselves apostasy from God, causing them to drink their own blood.

Through their idolatrous dealings, they failed to shepherd the flock of God faithfully. Concerned more with their nationalistic ideologies, they failed to uphold the Lord's commands to care for the fatherless and fight for the young and old mistreated under their watch. So the Lord sends the beasts of the earth to break down the whitewashed walls these church leaders thought would safeguard them.

They built walls of false prophetic protections for themselves, imagining they were in a spiritual paradise, where no harm would come to them. The leaders who supported idolatries had closed off their ears to the Lord, concerning themselves merely with their own desires while beating, chastising, and casting out the faithful brothers and sisters among them, taking no note of their own wrongdoing until their sudden collapse.

The Fourth Angel

Fourth Trumpet

Now, as John hears the fourth angel sound his trumpet, God's earthly organization is shuttered. On August 5, 2033, in fulfillment of the tenth of Av, the Lord's spiritual Holy Place on earth will be destroyed and cease to exist.

As the sun sets on this unfaithful church, the one-third that have remained faithful will see the lights that once were their spiritual guidance by day and by night go dark. The people are disbanded, the buildings sold off, and all will see its destruction for their errors. On this day, you will know it is by Jehovah God's Will that these things have come to be, as He is Lord of all whose judgments are righteous.

Fourth Bowl

For those who supported the idolatry within the church, the fall of the spiritual temple will be great torment to them. As our Lord Christ Jesus's face shines like the sun, so the fire of fulfillment on the tenth of Av will scorch those with anguish and grief who supported the adoption of the nationalistic adulteries, as their support structure comes crumbling down.

Even though these things come through the Will of God Almighty Himself, the people will curse His name, blaming Him for their iniquities as they continue to refuse to repent of their idolatries and deeds toward their fellow flock.

May our God and Father through Christ Jesus our Lord have mercy on all those who search Him out, and may they all have their clothes washed white in the blood of the Lamb in covering the shameful nakedness of sin.

A Call to Rebuild

On June 17, 2034, the two witnesses of God will present a call to rebuild the spiritual temple on earth. In preparation for our Lord's Coronation over the earthly kingdom sixty-nine weeks from this date, these two prophets of God will speak to great crowds where the prophetic Zerubbabel will declare God's Will of bringing back to Him a people under His name. As if dry bones are coming to life once again, great multitudes will hear the words of God and gather together in support of His kingdom on earth!

Be on the watch for Zerubbabel's message of establishing the foundation of God's earthly temple.

The Fifth Angel

Fifth Trumpet

In fulfillment of the remembrance days of Sukkot, from sundown September 27, 2034, to sundown October 4, 2034, will occur the collapse of governmental agencies comprising the first and second beasts of Revelation thirteen. In the crumbling of republics, an oligarchical society prepares itself for world domination in this first woe upon the earth.

At the collapse of these five nations into a proverbial abyss, John sees the angel of the Church of Laodicea, that fallen star, given a key by God, the One who holds the ability to destroy forever. After the angel opens the abyss, there comes out multitudes as scorpions with stingers that torment those without the mark of God placed upon them by Joshua, through the Capstone with the seven eyes. These people from all walks of life will declare the fulfillment of the fifth eye upon this stone after these governmental collapses.

As the sting of a scorpion agonizes the receiver, so too will the unfaithful be tormented by these powers of the two witnesses as fulfilled through the Capstone of the Lord. And with this message multiplying during this time, many videos and news articles will be recorded and remain in public view as metaphoric tales of scorpions over the next one hundred and fifty days, before the sounding of the sixth trumpet.

Fifth Bowl

As the fifth angel pours out his bowl on the throne of the wild beast, the republics collapse. The societies living within will be in agony and turmoil, not knowing what will come upon them next. Yet they will still refuse to repent and worship God Almighty, the Creator of all things. Instead, they continue to worship their idols of gold, silver, bronze, and clay bricks of demonic nations.

Peace be with you all, brothers and sisters, and may you remain faithful through the ever more trying days coming upon the earth. For great distress and woe are to come through the remaining two trumpets and bowls.

The Sixth Angel

Sixth Trumpet

The first woe upon the earth has passed, and now the second woe of the sixth trumpet and bowl have come.

As John witnesses the sixth angel sound his trumpet, the four angels who had been stationed before the Lord of the whole earth at the great river Euphrates are released to propagate their work of gathering His people to Him.

The faithful who are keeping away from the world and governmental idolatry are metaphorically killed to worldly concerns, like being refined in the furnace of the fires of judgment when these four craftsmen depicted on horses gather them together for the coming Coronation of the Lord Christ Jesus.

The unfaithful who refuse to repent of their idols of nations are not killed through the refining fires by these four angels but are instead prepared to be left behind. To be abandoned is to cease to exist forever.

Sixth Bowl

As the sixth angel pours out his bowl on the great river Euphrates, that barrier keeping the eighth and final demonic kingdom from arising out of the abyss is demolished, and that one-world oligarchy is established on earth, to be destroyed by the Lord at His Coming. Just as at the Tower of Babel, an oligarchy benefiting only a few yet presented as the answer to all of humanity's problems will declare itself as the way to world peace. However, as wolves in sheep's clothing, the true intent will be manifest through force and compliance by war.

    Remain faithful, dear friends in Christ, as you see these things come to be. Our Lord comes as a thief to remove one's name from the Book of Life only of those not keeping watch. Therefore rather, stay expectant of His arrival as He knocks upon the doors of those waiting and enters to share with us the Bread of Life if we remain in the faith and keep His commands.

The second woe has passed, and the third comes quickly at the sounding of the seventh trumpet and the pouring of the seventh bowl.

Part Four

The Seven Thunders

As John continues his record of the Revelation given him, he sees the Lord Christ Jesus Himself standing before him. Our Lord stands with one foot on the sea of humanity and the other on the land made up of the faithful. In Him are all the powers of judgment through redemption or condemnation. In His hand lies the unfurled prophetic scroll containing the mysteries given to His prophets such as Daniel, that come to their ultimate culmination at the sounding of the seventh trumpet. And as the angel who was speaking to John tells him to take and eat the scroll containing the fulfilled Word of God, it is as honey to the faithful, yet bitterly unpalatable to the unfaithful for whom destruction is prepared.

As John looks on in the vision, he hears seven thunders speak. These seven thunders are the seventh trumpet, seventh bowl, and first five seals. These seven all occur on October 13, 2035, in fulfillment of the remembrance day of Yom Kippur.

This is the day in the time of the end when Christ Jesus gains the kingdom of the earth and pours out His Spirit upon the faithful as He resurrects the dead of the elect as spirit beings. Ending the sixty-ninth week and beginning the seventieth on this day establishes the covenant for the kingdom promised to the elect, which Christ gave His disciples on the Lord's Day, designated at Passover.

Just as Christ Jesus experienced, the resurrected elect will remain on earth as spirit beings for forty days before their Lord appears in the clouds to collect them and the remaining still alive in the covenant position—all chosen to rule from the founding of the world.

The new covenant is confirmed through God's Holy Spirit when poured out on all of His people; the elect, as well as the great crowd, receive His Spirit on this very day. And through the awesome power of God's Spirit, the multitude will prophesy, dream dreams, and see visions as the elect shine like the sun.

But first, just before the sounding of the seventh trumpet, the star with the key to the abyss seizes the dragon, that liar, binding it in chains, and throwing it into the bottomless pit where it will be held for a thousand years, after which it will be let loose for a short period to deceive once again.

To all those living in that time, know this: The works of the dragon are to impersonate an angel of light. It is a demonic agenda that portrays the best interest of humanity separate from God's kingdom.

The Seventh Angel

Seventh Trumpet - First Thunder

At the blowing of the seventh trumpet comes the first thunder and third woe when our Lord Christ Jesus receives the kingdom of the earth on October 13, 2035, ending the 1,260 days. The seventh trumpet, seventh bowl, and first five seals all occur on this day in fulfillment of Yom Kippur, the holiest day in the time of the end.

May all Creation testify to the glory of God Almighty. Through His power, He has begun to rule. And through the Light that is the Life and Word, He will end darkness forever. It is time for judgment. Remain faithful, dear friends, so that you may receive your reward of eternal life.

Seventh Bowl - Second Thunder

As the seventh angel pours his bowl into the air, John hears the second thunder. The harlot city of Babylon the Great is divided into thirds when God's refined people come out from her captivity, establishing the new Jerusalem of the Lord on earth.

On this day, at Christ Jesus's Coronation over the earthly realm, the faithful third is confirmed when the Spirit of God is poured out upon them, the subjects of the kingdom, and the elect alike.

At the pouring out of the seventh bowl, as John peers inside, the temple of heaven is cleared of the smoke from the glory of God.

First Seal - Third Thunder

As John looks on in his vision, he sees the Lord as a Lamb approach His Father's throne and receive a scroll sealed with seven seals. The Lamb has the seven horns of refinement and the seven eyes of the Capstone, the luminaries sent out to be fulfilled in all the world.

And as the Lamb opens the first seal, the third thunder sounds, and one of the four angels, Christ Jesus, is seen being given His crown of rulership and sent out on a white horse to go behind the sea in preparation of judgments upon humanity.

Second Seal - Fourth Thunder

As the Lamb opens the second seal, the fourth thunder sounds, and the second angel rides forth on a fiery red speckled horse toward the nations of the world; as this angel takes peace away from mankind, war will now be great upon the earth.

Third Seal - Fifth Thunder

As the Lamb opens the third seal, the fifth thunder sounds, and the third angel begins his ride on a black horse carrying a set of scales. And as this rider goes forth, the eighth king takes control of national narratives. Although the eighth king may be able to indoctrinate the masses by a false agenda of world peace through destructive means, the true knowledge of God will remain available to those who seek it. Like the oil that feeds the lamps of God's Word, this Capstone of Scripture stands as the Revelations given to the prophets of God and fulfilled in their appointed time of the end!

Fourth Seal - Sixth Thunder

As the Lamb opens the fourth seal, the sixth thunder sounds when the fourth angel rides out on a strong pale horse; and its rider carries the name of Death. As this horse and rider go forth, great numbers of humanity will fall through war, famine, and plague. Many will perish through human hands from this day forward.

Fifth Seal - Seventh Thunder

As John continues in his vision, he sees the Lamb opening the fifth seal, as the seventh and final thunder is heard in fulfillment of Yom Kippur. And as he looks on, he records that he sees all the faithful elect from the Lord's Day on, resurrected to the earth as spirit beings. This is the first of two more resurrections to come. And forty days later, the Lord will appear in the clouds of heaven to collect them and the remaining 144,000 on November 22, 2035.

Forty Days

The fulfillment of Yom Kippur and the start of the forty days before Christ Jesus appears in the clouds of heaven ends the sixty-ninth week and the 1,260 days, bringing us to the seventieth. At the half of this week, the sacrifices of praise cease when the eighth king comes against the two witnesses and kills them. They will remain in public view, visible to all the world for three and a half days, at which point they will be resurrected before all eyes on October 20, 2035, ending this seventieth week. Then the nations will know their end is at hand.

As these two witnesses of God ascend to heaven, there will be a message broadcast from an angel, opening up the covenant for the kingdom to all. And he will say, "Fear God and give Him glory, for the hour of His judgment has arrived."

When the world sees these two prophets resurrected and hear this message of the kingdom go out to all, they will turn on the spiritual harlot Babylon the Great to destroy her. That demonic spiritual woman who rides the conglomerate beast will be burned and destroyed forever. She who killed the prophets and deceived the world through her idolatrous fornications will no longer harbor her lies, as she is torn apart and stripped naked, when death and destruction come upon her.

The Abomination

Ten days before the sixth seal is opened and the Lord appears in the sky, the eighth king will come against God's remaining elect on November 12, 2035, ending the 1,290th day from the removal of the sacrifices of praise from God. Thinking the Lord will pass by and leave this planet alone if they cut off Christ's remaining saints from the earth, they rise against those yet still alive to kill them.

On this day, the eighth king puts itself in place of God, requiring humanity to worship and support it in the battle against the Lord Christ Jesus and His elect. This will be the time of great tribulation upon the spiritual temple of God for ten days. Keep the faith and the commandments of God, and know that your endurance will bring about eternal life through the Lord, dear friends. When they are saying peace and security, sudden destruction will come upon them.

May you have the Spirit from the Almighty Father through our Lord Christ Jesus.

The Sixth Seal

On November 22, 2035, Christ Jesus will appear in the clouds of heaven, and all eyes will see Him.

At the opening of the sixth seal of this day, the sun will be darkened, and the moon will turn to blood. Ending the seven times from the beginning of the end, the Lord Christ Jesus will appear in the skies in preparation for the coming destruction upon the world. At this time, all humanity will hide in the rocks and caves of the mountains, hoping to protect themselves from the One seated upon the throne, for then they will know His great day of destruction has come.

Then our Lord will collect His 144,000 elect from all the earth. Those still alive at our Lord's arrival will be changed in the blink of an eye, and along with those resurrected forty days prior, they will all be caught up to meet Him in the clouds.

Let all of God's faithful enter their homes and close the door behind them until the wrath of God has passed. Fire will rain down upon the earth until the fulfillment of Hanukkah on December 28, 2035, when the spiritual temple making up all the world will be cleansed of all vileness, ending the seven solar years of the end and the sixth day, beginning the seventh-day rest of God.

The wild beasts that deceived the nations through their nationalistic ideologies will cease to exist forever, as God's kingdom crushes all these nations, casting them into a lake of fire that expunges completely all things thrown within, never to be seen again.

The Seventh Seal

After the 2,300 and 1,335 days are completed on December 28, 2035, the seventh-day rest and kingdom of our Lord begins when the temple of the earth is cleansed of all abominations.

And as John continues his account of the Revelation from Christ Jesus, he sees a large multitude from all nations coming out of the Great Tribulation dressed in white robes, cleansed through the blood of the Lamb in the forgiveness of their sins. And with symbolic palm branches in their hands, they praise God the Father through Christ Jesus to Whom they owe their salvation into the Promised Land. And the Lord will shepherd them and guide them to living waters, wiping every tear from their eyes.

As John looks on, he sees the Lamb open the seventh seal, and there is silence in heaven as the seventh day begins, a day of rest.

A Thousand Years

During this seventh day of God's kingdom, the Lord, along with His 144,000 elect, will resurrect many from the past to earth who either never had the opportunity to learn of God's redemptive grace while alive or require further instruction in His commandments. Many of those resurrected during these one thousand years will go on to eternal life (while some to eternal destruction when the dragon is let loose for a short period at the end of this seventh rest day). This is the second resurrection. The third will be all the faithful written in the Book of Life from the founding of the world after the thousand-year rest is completed.

The large multitude that John sees coming out of the Great Tribulation to God's kingdom, along with all the newly resurrected, will have the wonderful work of restoring the earth to that paradise lost in the Garden of Eden. Humanity will live in an idyllic paragon, where sin and death are no more. There will be no more sickness or infirmities or aging. There will be no more wars or suffering, for the entire earth will reside in peace.

Dear reader, hang on to what you have as precious treasure, for He is coming quickly.

New Heavens and New Earth

At the close of the thousand-year kingdom of God, the satan will be let loose from the abyss to go out to deceive humanity once again. This liar and deceiver will gather people under a humanistic ideology separate from God's rule once more. Again, people will be seen coming together in opposition to God's kingdom and those keeping the commands of God.

And when the numbers are full of those who will fall into slavery to sin at the end of these one thousand years, fire comes down from heaven, consuming them all. Then the devil, that accuser and slanderer who deceived those perishing, is cast into the everlasting fire, ceasing to exist forever.

Ending this seventh-day rest brings a close to the heavens and earth created on the second day from the world's founding. No longer will a barrier between God and man be needed, nor will there be any turbulent sea of peoples driven by the winds. There will no longer be a need to gather a people unto His Land, for all the world will be His.

Now the spiritual realm and the earthly will once again reside together.

The Book of Life

As the Lord opens the Book of Life after the thousand years are ended, all the faithful who had ever maintained the commandments of God throughout human history are resurrected into eternal life on earth. And all those not found in the Lord's Book are cast into the everlasting fires, never to exist again. This is the third and final resurrection and the second death.

After this, death and the grave of mankind are cast into those eternal fires. Never again will sin and death enter the world of mankind, for all the faithful shall go on to eternal life.

Finally, in the Revelation, John sees new heavens and a new earth, as the new city of Jerusalem comes down and resides with mankind forever. The metaphoric woman from the Garden of Eden who brought about the Lord's final separation of darkness from the light of His Will is seen now adorned as the new Zion, prepared as a bride before Him. God Almighty, now dwelling with humanity, brings flowing rivers of living water from His throne, as the healing powers of the Tree of Life fed by that river bear the fruit of eternal life to all those within the new city of God.

It is done! The Lord Christ Jesus is the Beginning and the End. He is the beginning of all Creation and the Light that ends darkness, sin, and death forever. No longer will the prophetic lights of prophecy be needed to light the path for His people, for God Almighty and the Lamb shall be their light eternally. And when all things have come to completion under the Lord Christ Jesus, He will hand the kingdom over to His God and Father Jehovah so that all things can be subject to Him, as He is all things in all.

Glory be to our God and Father Jehovah God through His Son Christ Jesus forever and ever. Amen

Repent and remain faithful to the commands of God, for He is close at the door!

www.ingramcontent.com/pod-product-compliance
Lightning Source LLC
Chambersburg PA
CBHW051829160426
43209CB00006B/1094